JUST AERNI'S BITTER BATTER BRAINS

for Amelie

BITTER BATTER BRAINS

Poetry and prose

by

JUSTIN AERNI

Edited by Desiree Willard

FRAGILE ARTIST

Uninhibited wishful thinking. On good days.
Unbearable gritty self-exploration.
Sanity at stake with every new venture.
Your fragile reality is but a falling egg. Ectoplasm soul
visually molested by all-consuming eyes and scrutinized.
Sweat shop messiah. Water into wine assembly line.
Most days.
Cast out cursed creator. You.
Hands like bricks. Your house will crumble.
And they expect it all for free. Every day.

NUNS ON LITHIUM

Bunched up old lilacs.
Pressed dried labia.
Laid on the single serve bed.
Fisting all together as one.
God head hallucinations and
sweaty medieval chastity belts.
Exhibit # A
Her burning bush.
Nightly miracles.
Miraculous climax.
Piano song in E minor.
Faith Renewed.
And the priest reads on and on.

THIS DIVINE MOMENT

Weeks . Months. Years waiting. Hoping.
Wet with rain and sea.
Hungry with untried passion and
thirsty with uncharted conquest.
Their young bodies first united
in the old broken telephone booth.
Their hormones awakened and
electrified by the passing storm.
Pressing together tight jeans and teenage lips.
Dreams of exhibitionism for him and Hollywood
romance for her. He was just a boy up until this
divine moment. The girl never knew she was a
woman until he touched her thigh.

The new lovers blessed and cured all the aliments
of the aging night with their bright youthful flesh.
In our own time we've all done our part to heal the night.
Making what was so very old new again and continuing the
human story.

YOUR HEAVY NAME

Honorably mentioned at every American
soldier's funeral. Your name. It was your name we heard,
and could your name be whispered in the cathedral halls
3000 years after the fact ? Taught to be feared and loved
by the many colored children on this earth indefinitely.
When holy and mighty ears on high stop hearing then
you must hear the screams of a frightened and lost
human race translated in every babel language
past and future.

Nailed face down to this work station desk that has become
your eternal cross. Hands and back whipped into consecrated
pulp by the devil. The whole world is waiting for you to listen
to their confessions now. If your ears are wide open then god
must be listening through you. I believe you could save every
last one of them if you could just keep that tired third eye
from closing tonight. Their rain tears hit you like a terrible
hurricane and you stumble around dizzy, barefoot and naked
carrying the heavy water weight on your worn serf back which
is now a modern sacrament held out on a shiny silver platter
for the hungry masses.

VACANT HOLOGRAM

Absent Phantom.
Superimposed sexual organs.
Midnight lust.
Rosary anal beads.
She gave him two black eyes.
Pistol whipped erection.
Cities full of mass murder and
other dark surprises.
Drown in this future.
2100 AD and going deeper.
Recorded transmission.
Not even there.
Chipped away.
UFO's to be corrupted data.
Fragmented abstractions of
shadow governments tie golden strings.
In the dark but never alone.

I USED TO BE A LOT OF THINGS

No traces left in those dusty pages..
I can't even remember looking now. .
This soul needs love girl. Real Love !
Screaming Love.. from .. well her name it's a
sin to even think it. I bow before her nakedness like
the first crucifix . No, not store bought but Roman made.
In this worship maybe I wept .. but only because I knew
we would meet in this spot again. I want to finally see her
tears. She promised me real tears!

We used to dance ..
Do you still remember ?
So slow that violin .. I was romantic back then.
Little revolutions ..Little spinning circles spun
deep in the small living room carpet.
I had fallen in love with the patron saint of
petty sex crimes but I was the one cast down.
While you were laying there naked in that manger
did you think of me ?.. Was it our little secret that
you could not forgive my self-destruction ?
I should offer you a birthday gift but.. I could
not even begin to give you all this lonely
solitude O' Lord.

CITY OF ROSES

Something simple.
Black or Brown.
Not too unusual or fancy.
Maybe wooden like the olden days.
No. Not padded.
Who cares if it's comfortable.
But before that , take me to the City
of Roses. Down on First Avenue.
By the quite glistening water
where I can sit in my last
hours and try to remember
her face and the most cherished
and intoxicated years of my life.

SHAVE THE CREATURES

Purifying ceremony.
The sex scissors shear.
A wolf's exposé.
Year after year.
Abundant the terror.
Simple herdsman unwittingly strike,
themselves here and there throughout
the night. The shaved creatures now
herdsmen up from all fours.
Their magic is black and their
faces are yours.

THE DESTRUCTION OF CANDY LAND

There was a man who drank cake batter. It was sacred to him. He shared with his many children this holy batter. They sat on the floor and partook of it out of a large silver mixing bowl. When their ritual was complete the family's long journey began. Shoeless, sock less and penniless they walked a thousand days over the many anchors of glass sugar shards. As they left I heard them saying, "Farewell. Farewell to your pseudo sophistication, forgotten innocence and your so-called candy hearts that chained and maimed the chocolate cherubs that once loved you. The cinnamon devils you call upon with vanilla alters of flesh walk under us now and strip away the skin under our feet. It is because of this we take your false tidings and combine them into one curse. One knife we direct back at you." As they left our city I could see the endless crimson river that followed. A river that cleared the cigarette smoke and cracked the temple mirrors and would come to wash away our once shining city… frosting and all.

MODERN AMERICAN ANIMALS

No strings attached is a rare thing.
Not to be wasted and hardly
ever happens twice in one's lifetime.
Met on flight coming home from Seattle.
Hot. Pink. Greased. Irresistible coastal meat.
We had no problem shedding the dull habitual
skins of modern American society and
showing our true. Brave and naked animalism.
Two caged tigers circling and sizing each other up.
Drooling and panting. Bowing down and biting.
Savage lapping. Heavy pounding followed by soft trembling.
Inside her consecrated womanhood I was everyone and
no one but most of all I was free.

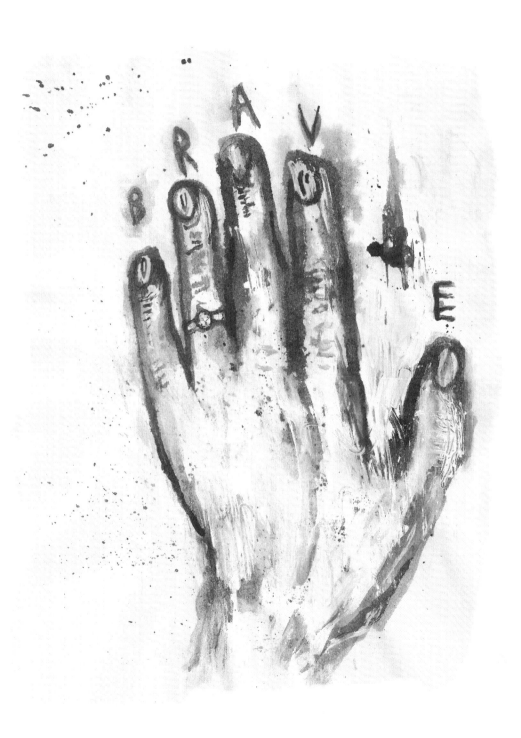

IF

If we wake up now.
If we go outside.
If we make love in the sunbaked field.
If we choose to be brave.
If we speak those timeless words.
If we really mean them.
Then our lives were worth living.

THIRD BASE

U _ _ _ _ _ _ your legs.
M _ _ _ your
P _ _ _ _ _ _ _ _ _ hands away.
I'_ waiting to see why I still play this
R _ _ _ _ _ _ _ _ _ game.
E _ _ my madness. Let it breathe.
   Don't be modest, don't be smart.
   Just spread that bashful slit apart.

ALLISON'S BREASTS UPON ME

Allison's perfect teenage breasts exposed and at the ready. Bringing me to complete amnesic paradise again. When I'm awake I grow nostalgic and sometimes jealous over their soft sexual phylactery and the sadistic power they hold over me. Their pressure bearing down on me becomes erotically unbearable. I can feel the shameless erection of your two sex circus tents and suddenly my thoughts become thirsty. Smother me. Smother me now with your mounds of doughy flesh. I want you to push me deeper into this self-imagined coma. If I wake up now I will surely die.

YOU

I'm not claiming to be smarter than you.
I mean I'm a fucking idiot for all intents and purposes.
Really! That didn't even really make sense...

But enough about me.
I don't matter.
I want to know more
about you my love.
What kind of garbage have
you had to sift through to find truth in your life?
How's that opposable thumb working out ?.. Pretty tired by
now right ? Did you know as a small child that unlike
other animals in the zoo the rules didn't apply to you ?
This is not some overblown , over publicized and grandiose
experiment in 21st century literature. This is me..
Little old me, trying maybe
failing to penetrate you.

Let's reach deep past the sovereignty
of your outer core. I want to swim like a god
in your lust.. Your childhood fears ..
I want to know where you
think you'll end up when you're dead.
I want to be in you.
In the purest of fashions of course.
Unless you really want to play.

THIS MAN'S JOURNEY

This is one man screaming into the abyss.
This is one man setting out across your unforgiving wilderness.
This is one man who cannot .. no will not say goodbye.

So is there a reason for all of this ?
I reach out for your embrace ..
Hands old and heavy with ancient chains.
Fingers like iron anchors . Monsoon tears held back but
I'm drowning just underneath the surface when you say;

This journey has made you ugly.
This journey has made you rough .
This journey has made you tired.
This journey has made you old.

You stand perfect as an ivory pillar and
silent as a blank page in the royal
doorway and look down indifferent to my suffering.
I know now it was never enough .
This journey has taken me places Dante would fear to tread.
He's back at base camp praying and yet it was not
enough to win your heart but I guess you were expecting armies.
You were awaiting a private coach while I offer a lowly work mule.

Oh god how naive I was..

GOD GOON WRATH

Staring down. His eyes locked on my eyes. His cold alien eyes straight down on me. In me. My thought crimes revealed and publicized throughout the heavens. The prepubescent colossus does not contemplate ending me, he just does. Equal to or less than a bus of Christian school children he steps on with shallow indifference. Clumsy fucking child. Here comes the son. Mr. Jesus CEO. The dumbfounded despot. The goon that saved you from yourself and kept you wishing on a star.

SILENT WAS THE SNOW

Do you remember the way you felt standing there on
top of your compacted snow tower.. The city bus
should have been here twenty minutes ago and you're
still looking up hoping it doesn't stop any time soon.

The silence all around you. In you.
Your Muse. Your god. Waking in this
frozen moment created for you. The
delicate flakes glisten and seem to
stop just below the yellow street light.
Hopelessly abandoned,
yet somehow comforted
in your winter haven.

THE ENTHUSIASTIC DISCIPLE

I bow before her backside and silently worship.
This naked monument to my sexuality
seen with undeserving dog eyes.
The pose greater and stronger than any
Colossus of Rhodes. The entrance
more magical and heavenly
than any Buddha or Jesus.
Her lotioned feminine skin
like heavily guarded and
polished museum sculpture.
The arch of her back surpassing
any golden Roman key stone.
She is my religion and I am her
loyal martyr.

BLUE SAND

We were the breeze.
You on your arthritic knees.
Myself so young and eager to please.
You lapped up my boyish milk heart from the saucer.
I watched on as my youth was urgently devoured.
Time, the enemy that would steal you away.
Decades spent. Our children grown.
The yellow paint chips falling from our home.
Like some kind of breeze we came and went.
Our love in an hour-glass.
Our blue sand a winter snow storm
supplanted by the coming spring.

HELL AS A ROOM

Sick man dies.
Sinking stiff.
Unclean breakaway.
Downward drift.
Falling cellular trash.
Blind eyes see.
Interlocking black & white tiles.
Sinister and surrounding.
Stealing life from
the already dead.
Fighting yourself
as an enemy and
something else I think
is in this room with me.

VICTORY TO THE SUN LORDS

Revamped again was our bitterness well deserved and sought after. None a greater show of death was achieved before that day. Our long war was finally lost against the most high sun lords that now sought to murder us all from the heavens above.

Finally we would be earning the scars we had longed for all those years. The weaker ones among us were praying for this final reckoning and release from pain. Knowing this the two remaining nations with kings and clergy hidden deep like moles in the earth set a plan in motion and sent their many blood hounds unto the outer tribes to gather up all the virgins. To each man were forty and two virgins. Now with both contingency plans in place they set forward into the burning sky. Two charities I saw and then the ground began to thunder and split in two. Massive burning charities of steel and light like great swords they cut through ash cloud and star-dust. When they finally cast the stars down on us, I could not believe the spectacle. With only moments left I witnessed a billion brazen souls rise up out of their graves with mouths open as if they could swallow their own annihilation. Any hope and dream of a future was now just a speck in the sky.

BITTER BATTER BRAINS

These bitter batter brains tainted and
forever over complicating the very simple.
Poisoning young impressionable minds and
mixing all the perfect colors of sky and
earth into fecal mud.

A neuron structure more impassable and
disconnected than any M.C. Escher drawing.
Walking forward but wanting backwards.
Following intelligent lemmings to high mountain
cliffs and falling with the best. Waiting for an
appointment with an over scheduled and over
worked Jesus CEO. Out of breath and advice
for your 21st century. Take my last lucky liberty
coin and put it in your holy little pocket.
Shake lose your snake skin smile and frown
at me like Pierrot in his prime.

Let's strive to be more real .. more truthful than any
celebrity gossip magazine. I want to fly higher than
the bravest and strongest of emperor penguins.
I will remember you more clearly than any
stage three Alzheimer's / Amnesia patient.
I'll run away with you just after this quick
leg amputation and I'll pray with you just
after the last unanswered prayer has
been answered.

HAPPINESS IS SIMPLE

Jamie wrote out all her lonely memories in hopes of healing.
Kimberly wrote about the day her beautiful daughter was born.
Tim wrote down everything he ever loved in hopes of letting it all go.
Mary wrote about the men who took away the best years of her life.
Jane wrote down every instance she reached out for love and found none.
Kevin wrote down the hard times that made his soul grow.
Jason wrote down every time he thought he wasn't good enough to
breathe. Christopher wrote about the time his father saved his life.

Kathy wrote down her weekly grocery list and smiled...

TNIAS

I carved. Tears fell with the stigmata blood.
My youthful blood.. seemed purer than yours.
For hours I carved in front of that ugly mirror.
Carved what you always dreamed me to be in
my own flesh. The only thing that would get
me through those pearly gates was that one
unobtainable word.. The word that represented
everything I could never be. You probably mistook
me as a martyr. I understand. It was very frightening.
The path to god .. well your god is a tight rope and
I am an untrained and unbalanced circus performer.
Terribly afraid of heights. Distracted and holding a
heavy death wish in my left hand..

...but maybe I was the ugly one and not the mirror..

FROZEN TEARS

Every memory comes back to an image of a lowly father holding
a newborn child. Barely breathing and struggling for a place in this
world. The father's hands are cut and freezing as he toils in the
winter snow to provide. The flakes are like acupuncture needles
that pierce his face and unforgivably push in deeper with each
working hour , making him always remember the night of pain
and heavenly wrath. My boy.. My boy... He cried;

My baby boy's spirit has blown far away, carried up forever into the
cold December air and I can never hope to find him among the heavy
downfall. No .. too broke for a proper funeral he was burned cheap.

It's enough to make your fucking heart stop. That was
1984 and no one ever said the pain of losing
a son was worth living through.

LETTERS LIKE DAGGERS – LOVERS LIKE SCARS

Comets like rain. An end of an age.
Letters sealed with a kiss. Nothing to miss.
She's trying to forget the letters that I sent.
My words embedded deep. Crying herself to sleep.
Like shrapnel they tear our lingering love affair.
She's trying to forget the truth in my pages.
The love I had for her. Time can't erase it.

You wanted to know the truth and how our love fell apart.
It beings at the top of the page where the first line starts.
Like Murder Mouse I'll stick a dagger in your heart.
Letters like daggers. Lovers like scars.
To you love is getting fucked in the back seat of a car.

MY LIFE AS A BLUE BIRD

Falling almost floating.
Soft blue feathers reach out fearless.
Joyous sacred spirals. Dive spin.
Muscles aching. Skinny white spine flexing.
The invading giants stare up with envy at my
childish mastery.

I could die as a wild youth.
Brilliant and worthless ... but less
superior in their eyes .
Or if they wish I could
feed forever from thick sweaty palms ..
Grow old and regretful behind thin
mass produced Auschwitz bars as an equal.

A LETTER TO A.

Dear A,

My love and muse for life.
You chose me to be your dad this time.
Why you did. I cannot know.
But because you did I've grown.

I think we met before a thousand years ago.
Playing hide and seek in Roman streets.
Maybe I was the child and you were the mother.
I guess I forgot. You were always more clever.

Back then people were wild animals, terrible and huge.
You were the only one brave enough to give them their dues.
I dreamt you were smiling on the face of the moon.
Somewhere I could never go but maybe you can soon.

You were made to do great things. A masterful creation.
The power to feed the world or bring it to annihilation.

Destined to free the oppressed of a broken generation.
Keep your head up girl. Now I don't pretend to know what you're facing.
Just keep on believing in yourself and keep asking those hard questions.
Daddy's always with you. I'll be there by your side.
Even after this worn out body dies.

~ Daddy.

THE LAST TREE WE EVER CLIMBED

Climbing up this endless memory together.
Our thoughts intertwine raising us up by divine tree roots.
Clouds and stardust cover the ground now and there's no
other way but up. My sister and I share the vines that lead
up into the velvet blackness of space or maybe it's heaven
because that would explain the tears in our eyes and the
many bells ringing in the far distance.

Higher and higher now we can see figures flying and waving
at us from overhead bringing with them pure light and angelic
singing. Like ancient magic we become weightless and with
childish little smiles we look at each other as we both let go
of the earthly branches knowing that we will never come down.
Knowing finally that we've made it.

MY NEW GIRLFRIEND

Do Do Do.. Dot Dot. Due Do DO Do.Dot Dot.

Pretty little ghost. Compassionate silent lover.
Such a playful little thing. My soft semi-gloss gargoyle.
Glancing behind her naked left shoulder she sees into me.
Transparent yet radiant. Horrifying yet hypnotizing.
Exposed and Frozen in place. You and now me with fear.
Pushing these mortal eyes back deep into safe warm sockets.
I want to be your frightened fleshy boyfriend.
I need sweet spirit kisses and I need you to
hold me with your invisible arms when I'm deep inside you.
I know I should get someone
breathing but I think.. no I'm
sure it's better this way.

Do do do Dot Do...

INSOMNIA < COMATOSE

Momma is up late.
Checks baby for breath.
Time = Total reversal.
Now you're worried to death.
You're checking her again.
Up late drinking wine.
Useless unproductive hours.
God's sick gift for you tonight.
The solitude of midnight.
Insomnias unbearable breath.
You wish this for your mother
but she's comatose instead.

THIS IS ME SENDING ALL MY LOVE TO YOU

You there.
Reading with that smug little grin.
Fuck You. I see you. . Or see through you.
You would devour me if I was just a little
more delicate in your mouth. Don't pretend
you were not the one who lynched that poor
soul on First Street. You showed us all that day..
The blood almost touched your merciful
white gloves. Don't pretend to give a shit
about trying to figure this all out. Just put
me down and pretend you actually finished
something like you always say you do.
Mr. Holier Than Thou. I can see you now
with your pocket messiah and your failed
Socratic philosophy. Man was meant to be
broken and if you choose to fall to your
knees besides me as a complete failure
then maybe we can read and struggle
on together.

THESE WORDS CAN NEVER BE SHARP
ENOUGH FOR WHAT YOU DESERVE

My old father. Years flew.
Tongue cut out by his daddy and he was
speechless for fifteen years. Dogma, an
old man's comfort blanket.
He raps himself up tight.

He tries to bury his sins in the ground.
His soul a waste bucket of regret.
Blessed and cursed by all his forsaken lovers.
His lust was legend. He passes down the shame
to his unwanted children. My young sister sleeping
there in the corner. I remember. I can see her
innocent eyes looking up at this so called ...Man.

I used to think you were Jesus. Did you know ?
Your escapism .. your cowardly sensitivity.. cuts
deep into your own flesh which you quickly bandage
with dirty pit money. This is your legacy.. not mine.

VICTIMLESS CATCALL

Throw your lust at the world.
Tell that girl how you really feel.
Sweetheart, curves need love songs too.
I give this to you free because I wanna screw.
Baby, Baby my eyes have seen the light.
She looks young, pink and mighty tight.
(WHISTLE WHISTLE)
Hey Sexy!

JUST UNDERNEATH

Subterranean ant empires.
Unexplored and restless these
hidden and hallowed out dark worlds.
Monster matchmakers and self-described
undead animators working tirelessly in the
cold dirt. Self-reliant in their own way yet
dependent on the flood waters to wash
down every spring and fall. There is a
rumbling in the ground now. Two great
and terrible feudal armies marching.
The loud clang and clashing of bronze
shields and bloody xenomorphic swords.
Lords and kingdoms rise and fall
every day just beneath our
unsuspecting feet.

THE MEMORY OF YOU

Branching out like
those falling whisper sounds. .
When we were kids we would
sit and listen to the ones that
hid behind the trees.
Nothingness.
The Nothingness of you.

Shy memory . Frozen. Falling with you .Now Fading ,
Still Harmonizing .. soft tones as I lay down with you.
The girls all laugh but I had this vision .. This vision
only an echo to you. Swimming and swooshing
around inside this top heavy human skull.

They spoke to us there.

LONG DISTANCE HEROIN

I call this certain number every single night. I pay using CC
and they shoot me up tight. Through my eardrums and in
my brain the drugs did go. I get so high when the sounds
start to flow. The cops can't bust me because the numbers
off shore. I'd like to thank A.Graham Bell for putting me
back on the floor. Immersed now in what was never
humanly imagined. Ambient was the celestial noise, full of
sexual abandon. With one phone call my ailments cured.
Sound is orgasmic when you're high as a bird.

HAPPILY MARRIED

The lonely and rejected are left to examine
their own empty nakedness in the ugly light
of each cold morning. With uneasy companions
of tears and expensive foreign cigarettes they sit
under the high bridges. So high and isolated they
stare down upon all the lovers of this world and
whisper desperate gypsy curses through chapped lips.

Closer to god and nature in this way
they are only touched and fondled by
the harsh wind and rain. Strangely
Holy but sinfully alone. Blessed
with serene solitary and cursed
with the resentfulness of an old
aroused priest. Placing the promise
rings on the familiar left and right.
The praying position of fingers
causes the gold pieces to meet
and clang with some kind of sick
exuberance. The marriage of
one's self to one's self is done
privately in messy apartment
bedrooms with curious ghosts
and sometimes apathetic feline
witnesses. The consummation
of this pact; ritualistic and well
known since early adolescence.
The honeymoon a lavish trip to
Maui you saw that night on TV.

LIE

The pain experienced and shared
by the living can only exist in one's mind.
Therefore we are just a species being
held together by this simple lie.
Just a desperate illusion and a way
to cope with the overwhelming loneliness
that shows itself as the great abyss
we are all thrown into at childhood.
Complete enlightenment mastered
only before we take our first breath
and then as we are torn screaming
from the peace and serenity of
our mothers we can only wait now
to return to the time that we
were better. Perfect. Without law.
Without crime. Without the slow
degeneration of our own self loathing
thoughts. Free from the endless guilt
brought on by years of brain washing
by any and every dogma your parents
have chosen to instill in you and finally the
illusion of pain. The great preposterous
lie that binds and slowly destroys us all.

FAMOUS FACIAL: AN AMERICAN NOVELTY

Made in America. Copyrighted ©. Trademarked ™.
Patented ®. Mass produced , photographed and televised.
Our glorious creation. The pride of a nation. A nostalgic
pastime.

SEA FOOD RIOT

Anorexic kings and other malnourished royalty flood the street.
Feudal scavengers bust out Asian shoreline market windows. The
duke of Pompano with his Turbot knights collect what's left on ice.
Hoarding the Alaskan crab and scampi bags. Cursing the fat
totalitarian peasants that oppressed and starved them for all those
generations.

REGRETFUL THRUST

Skin flaps fully extended and moist. Nerve endings protracted and electrified. Bulbous and ballooned were the soft exterior openings. Parasympathetic engine oiled and massaged into working order. I heard the two personages moan with the roar of a whole continent, an entire people crying out with lustful anticipation. I was planet XXX. The other just a helpless young planet earth caught up in a deadly fixed orbit confrontation. With this prolonged motion and one final regretful thrust it was all over too soon and the conception was complete.

THE OUTSPOKEN FLEA

Stuck in a town named after a city.
Full of gigantic pistol whipping cowboys
and prehistoric red farmers. Big back wood
brutes and half crazed alcoholic truck drivers.
Cigarette stained teeth, rodeo trophies and pop
country music pressing down. Oppressing.
Confining. Surrounding. Choking. Exterminating.

Got real drunk off of redneck martinis and shot
the old mouth off again. Heavy lumberjack fists fly.
The familiar taste of the gravel parking lot. Black eye
earned carelessly. Police siren echo. Hurry. Get up on
your skinny insect legs and stumble back into the dark
alley from which you came.

FEMALE

Just wait.. You just wait princess.

In a couple decades oh worshiped one, we shall see whose smiling.
You used your beauty as a weapon against the weakness of men.
The fact is my love, time is on my side and wasn't it you who told
me that men get more defined with age and women just get
more haggard ?
So in midlife the playing field is finally even and in the years after
the scales tip in our favor. My chauvinism is minuscule compared
to your female manipulation and sex crimes. No. No. Not crimes
to you but means of barter. This is your unsightly future ... Female.
So enjoy the power while you can still command our hearts
and wallets.

The fact is my love I've waited all my life to tell you this.

YOUR CHILD MISSING YOU

To: J. Aerni

Dear Selfish Coward,

While you waste away in your mother's basement, she is missing you. She will wonder where you are when she falls asleep tonight just like every night. Now you are out gallivanting in another town up north and she is thinking about you. Each tear you can't wipe away becomes a mark against you. Every time she reaches out for daddy and you're not there is a self-inflicted holocaust. But she's forgetting all about you now and above all else you fear this the most.

Sincerely;

J. Aerni

YOUTH

As a little child easily envisions
impossibly perfect day dreams
we too can look back with
longing and remember how
beautiful we once were.

Our dreams like far-fetched horizons,
brightly colored and just
enough space for those endless wheat
fields to sooth our restless newborn souls.
As a child everything is slowly burning and floating.
Every minute is magic like an undiscovered word.
Don't be afraid to stand close to the
vast expanse of eternity because
time is kind to the very young.

The curious flickering of ideas like the restless
feathers of a hungry humming bird.
Closer to heaven than earth. Furthest from
death than you could ever know.
Even Methuselah stands over you with deadly
envy and is threatened by your innocent longevity.
So cherish that youthful soft glow and the love for life
that comes so easy when you're all brand new.

CHEERS

Cheers to all the useless women that have stolen
away the best years of my life. To every shallow
materialistic bitch who decided that I was not
good enough. For every kid who pushed me
down and made me swallow rocks. Yes you.
Angelic you. I have not yet forgotten your kind
lessons oh holy and enlightened ones. The world
must be a beautiful place because it's full of saints
like you. It's these sacred tragedies that keep my
finger on the trigger of this proverbial gun. Feel
the cold steel against your temple. It was this and
only this that you taught me. How could I ever pay
back this deep debt I owe you ? Should I expose
your soft nakedness ? Your hidden crimson ink.
I would love to show the world the colors of your
perfect souls.

REQUIEM OF THE DEMONIC JUVENILE

Puts his head way down. Almost hidden. Almost not there at all. Learns to be deceptive. Cunning. Wants to set the world on fire. Hatred finds him. Wants at the same time to be loved. Invisible now to the teachers. Walks home with head down. Always down. Sits in the dark writing this down.

10/29/2001

SAINT AERNI STRIKES AGAIN

I'm much too quiet now almost mechanical.
Whatever her name was ? , she's picking up on my self-loathing now.
I look straight through her to the white pillow her head is resting on as I
finish. My obvious self-loathing in this act is her humiliation.

Sitting naked on a dirty bed wearing nothing but
a cheap condom. With the sweat and smell still
on me I've already thought about this mistake a
thousand times. The shame slowly hitting me
in waves like the first minutes of fear , anger
and frustration of finding out that you have
terminal cancer with just a couple months to live.

Similar minutes of awkward silence have passed
and she's already gone without a kiss or a
"I'll call you." So how could I become so
detached from something that is so
personal ?

"I wasn't put here to be your hero baby", I think to myself.

No.

Some of us were born to play the super villain and knowing
this from a very young age gave me an advantage over the
kingdom of ants at my feet and the Lilliputians hiding in
my shadow. We are all born with generic names based off
of pop culture icons and dead relatives but some of us later
in life choose our own names. She didn't.. Maybe that's why
I cast her out with my eyes. I wanted her to hate and fear me
much like I do myself. I've come to learn that these names are
more significant and closer to our true nature than the shallow
names given at birth. Mine was written in blood which I hear
lasts longer than ink.

CASTRATED – OVERRATED YANKEE

Born up north. Hazleton Pennsylvania.
Fat kid complex but the critics can't blame ya.
I liked you better when your art had balls.
When your shit was scribbled out , iconoclast,
burnt up and off the fucking walls.
You talked a lot smack and some people
even praised you. Seriously now. I don't think
you even believed you. You picked a fake name
so the world couldn't find you. So egotistical
now the devil's way behind you. This isn't
sour grapes, I just call it like a see it.
History is proving you to be extremely overrated.

GOING OUT IN STYLE

Woke up in a different world today.
A world that was no longer safe to call mine.
Rubbed the sleep out of my tired eyes this morning
with handfuls of worthless cash and combed my own
grey hair to prove I had earned it. I in fact had earned
the end. This romantic farewell. Everybody's..

I can hear the neighbors I never cared to meet packing
and screaming at each other. I'm leaving too you know..
but I don't know where I'm going. Why does this last day
have to be so damn warm and bright ? The criminals dress in expensive
black riot gear and have finally given up the spirit
of entrepreneurship for a steady government paycheck and a
cheap yellow badge. I can hear them coming now. Systematically. House
by house they become faster , robotic, numb and more proficient. Maybe
I should set my house on fire and give them something pretty to look at.
Maybe I should set myself on fire
like those brave Buddhist monks and give them something
to remember.

88

BEGINNING EARTH

In the first beginning before the beginning you've read about.
Before the reign of death. Before a man's thoughts were just
his own. There ruled a great sorceress and within her was
the great heartbeat of our young fetal planet. Every night
she knelled down on the edge of the world. Hands clasped
and Jesus beaten. Half sedated and dying. With a dazed
kind of messy Aramaic magic whisper on her lips.
Her simple sorcery had kept the entire planet
alive for another day. This gift she gave freely.
And it was my job to keep her always wanting.
Explaining all the reasons to keep us all breathing.
Worshiped by the many curious angels that flew by
and hated amongst the lower earthbound demons
and suicidal religious fanatics. Back in those days
we shared a small wooden hut. There was no need
for clothes for we knew no shame. Every night we
would make love and her skin would glow like a neon
crucifix. There were whole centuries of endless pleasure.
Each night after her selfless sacrifice she became weak so
I would hold her in my arms and feed her fruit from the garden.
Eventually her glow had faded into darkness. After our short millennium
together she was gone. That night I braced myself
for the destruction of the planet but instead it was we who died. Mankind
Inside. And in my last moment connected I realized
she was actually praying for us.

SUNFLOWER DUNGEON

Sprinkled.
Subtle.
Afternoon light.
Salvation come down from the blue window.
Elusive afterthought.
This left luminary path.
Cotton like bricks against the battered labia.
Grasping – Resisting. Dim glimpse.
And once again … Elusive.
And you fall far behind her in quivering introspection.

BECKONING OF THE DEMENTED

Would you come and help me navigate the vast oceans of pain?
Do I go on bleeding while my lover's off screwing? I have finally
come home feeling a million miles away. With my children left
behind I fear they'll soon forget my name. How can one breathe
in a world that is drowning? How can one sleep when there are mouths to
be feeding? Today I wept thinking of you. The girl lost
in a manufactured paradox. Begging for answers from a mute god. She's
my catatonic sunflower. My concealed sexual transaction.
The lip candy I eat with crushing victory.

REMEMBER THE LEECH

Supply and demand.. Supply and demand.
Secret warehouses full .. Distributed carefully
and incrementally. As the demand goes higher
more blood is spilled.

Accountants transcribe these quarterly profits in blood.
Each number is its own mini tragedy. Each business year
a holocaust. The global machine that keeps us safe and
warm and everyone else starved and annihilated.

Our success has left us empty.
Look at us now. Two imposter robots.
Two struggling pillars shaking beneath
the weight of our own greed and immense
egos. Disintegrating and destructive.
Beautiful and untouchable.

.. Ignore that last part.

HOLY SMOKE AND MIRRORS

No mask on your face.
There is no place.
To hide. Survive.
From the Son, The father &
The holy smoke and mirrors.

To thy O' lord I offer just a taste.
The cruel medicine that you create.
Patent.
Distribute.
Shake well. Take it every Sunday.
Angels on street corners.
Celestial Hustlers.
Empire of fear.
Profits heaven high.

So much hurt.
So much crime.
So many ridiculous biblical lies.

Created the devil.
Offered yourself up as the solution.
The dysfunctional paradigm you sell to the Lilliputians.
Crucifix tattoos. Holy water amulets. Selling Jesus
as a millionaire. I can't believe it's come down to this.

ON A HAPPIER NOTE

Sacred insecurities past down
lovingly from mother to child.
The tragedies of this world converge
deep down and corrupt the boy's infant heart.
Born too brave to last. Died like a bitter Jesus
with a cease and desist letter from daddy hidden
in his loincloth. World wars and natural disasters
just destinations on humanities burning road map.
The bodies of a million slain are the trophies of any
memorable human century. Trillions spent marketing
fear porn. Holy signs of our new and upcoming
Hollywood apocalypse reality show appearing.
Watch attractive young "un-stars" make real
revelation drama in the end of all days.
The ratings will be biblical. Any important thing
that you thought you might have done or remembered
for simply forgotten, washed away or burned back into
the black hole nonexistence from which it came.

On A happier note , Tommy got an "A" on his
math test today...

WASTELAND FRONTIER

Empty cold side of the bed.. I dare not touch you.
Her smell remains but it's just a hurtful tease.
Hair curlers, an old blow dryer, mascara and
crumpled up movie tickets are the relics of
what's left of her and the love that once was.
The hole she left has no conceivable bottom.
I must find some way to fill the long hours of
the day. I must become an explorer. I must
travel this wasteland frontier of our shared
memories. To try to find an answer. The way out.
I lost everything that mattered in one swift
downward chomp. One wretched summer night.
Everything beautiful in my life just gone. Gone. Gone.
But I can't blame the poor girl. There's more wet baggage
here than on the sinking Titanic. My fear has made
me a loser. Unworthy of a long, happy, boring life with her.
No. Instead I must have a short, melancholy, interesting
life alone. How can one love such a freshly
wounded failure? How does a man go on and on
and on existing without a point? Was man made
to struggle every damn day until the day
he drops dead?

MY HEART IN A GLANCE

Pretty little thing waiting there.
With an innocent look she attracts my hungry stare.
Such a sleek youthful face.
Flesh, bright and swollen. I need a taste.
My eyes on you like super glue.
You're bewitching my soul. You're taking me captive.
Your soft pale eyes could control the masses.
Please meet my glance like the chosen few who
wore the shackles of love just to be with you.
I'm on my knees for your sweet touch.
Your heart-shaped hips mean so much.
Your body a fruit, pure and delicious.
My heart in a glance you fail to witness.

~ Fighting For Fiction. 2008.

PACT

It could be romantic.
It would be nice to end
with you by my side.
We could listen to those Leonard Cohen
songs you told me made you cry.
We could eat everything
we always wanted without shame.
We could help each other forget about
this cold unforgiving world.
We could even hold hands if
that's how you want them to find us.
We could lie down and dream forever.

FEAR, BRICK AND MORTAR

Zero eye contact means less forced
human interaction / conversation.
There's something strangely satisfying
about hiding under your desk at work.
Examining your boss's brown penny loafers
and the confusion in his voice when he thinks
you're not there.

What's even better is when you make a little
fort in your bedroom closet. You can live safely
in there. Don't forget to bring your TV, food and
some reading material. Later on if you feel like
that closet needs a lock you can have someone
buy one for you. When that lock is not enough
you can have them wall you in with brick and mortar.
When what's on that TV becomes too terrifying you
can sit in the dark. When that darkness becomes too
lonely you can sleep. No one will be able to hear you
or even know you exist. You'll get what you
always wanted!

In a hundred years they'll find your bitter ashes and
an old copy of this book.

THESE BRAIN(S)

R-A SUICIDE

. GOOD GOD

It's the children you sold to the devil and the begging heard
from his jaws. It's the 1980's nostalgic pornography pages
your semen is stuck upon. It's the diseased sewer rats that
will never see the sun. The asshole that hit your cat and
laughed just for fun.
A heritage of hate. A passed down southern song.
The blanket of saliva. The only one that keeps you warm.
Your fisting patron. His German switch blade. The metal
on your thigh. An autopsy photograph of Elvis that
conspiracy theorists deny. The mischievous mortician that
plays with your dead mother's breasts. Your January belly.
The fit teenage enemy that rubs it in your face.
The redneck cracker that stole your fickle girlfriend away.
The catastrophic fall of Babylon. America is next they say.

REINCARNATION

Countless past lives will make you bitter.
I worked too hard and died too often.
I decided this life will be my revenge.

OBLIVIOUS VINCENT

Postmortem fame was the
price you paid for putting
down your Bible and
picking up a paint brush.
And here we are a hundred
years later still in
astonishment over
your fatal decision.

STONING J.

Three years in. Oops! Now we got a problem.
She can't stop singing about her lonely oppressed vagina.
A liberated woman is who she wants to be.
Tension in the rose garden. Her sexual malnutrition.
A violent take over he never thought could be.
A private democracy is just a tyranny in a slutty outfit.
Uncontrollable her itch. She started stepping out on him.
She undressed for seven that summer and her man was
never the wiser.
Feeling her way through her many lover's trousers.
With some guilt she severed her own head up on a platter.
He forgave her then but she was back out screwing in an
hour. So with these spiteful words we stone her forever.

ATONING DEVIL

The devil sleeps on my couch.
He shaves almost daily and smells
of rosemary and mint. During the
day you can find him outside feeding
the ants sugar and whispering over them.
When it's raining he sits up in the dark
sewing room and sings softly to the caged
finches there. He eats all our unwanted
leftovers and every Sunday he drinks
cheap fruit wine from the corner store.
He often lectures the family on the
importance of life insurance and how
he wants to be my agent. Then he said
he could take me to New York City to
make me a big star. Sometimes he would
take me out driving at night and talk about
how he forgot how to lie. I mean I like him
as a roommate and all but now that I'm
older I can take care of myself.

NO LONGER LOST

When I was lonesome I would talk to the
mighty gorillas that lived up in the misty hills.
When I was dirty I bathed with the enormous
hippos and leaches to get clean. When I was
hungry I sharpened my spear and caught my
own seafood. During the night I dreamed of
living in the big city and during the day I day
dreamed of being eaten by large predator cats.
In the winter I would burn my fire with crab tree
bark and during the summer I would gather old
bamboo to make signal fires. Hopelessly lost and
alone. I struggled to survive every single day.
Finally feeling free and with a purpose , I
stopped gathering bamboo.

STATUE OF MISERY

Oxidized feminine hands.
Chained to the great lie.
Inescapable cumulative guilt.
Her messy historic entanglement.
The imagined French child prostitute
modeled after a carbon copy Greek goddess.
The body.
Our gift shipped in pieces.
Voracious hands.
Hands that now stretch around the world.
Clenching every neck and dollar.
Her/Our misery inflames the world.

SPOKANE

Tortured blue vein.
Illegal drug super highway.
Pain. Pain. Self-inflicted pain.
A town full of stuck up losers.
Cardboard box hideouts and
RV meth labs. Crooked carnival
cops. Eight months of winter.
Mediocre Mormon Mini Malls.
Hells Angels , God's beloved shit
kicking born again sinners. Hang
over vomit smeared into passed
down brown corduroy jeans.
Bullshit blues makes me think
of Spokane. Time wasted.
An entire generation of ungrateful
assholes. Pretenders, Suicidal Clowns
and amateur porn stars.

The town I love to hate.

LOYAL LOVER. IT'S TOO LATE.
MUCH TOO LATE.

Trying to listen in on your lover's phone calls now.
This is a new tradition for you. She packed a simple
lunch for you. She completed this task without your
Thank you or smile. When will you buy her that
promise ring and push those other threats out for good.
You've grown tired and lazy and they have grown restless
and will soon swoop quickly in after her with wild romantic
notions and new hypnotizing sexual exploitations.
Anyone looking for love can choose to be hunted.
Only a few can be trained to resist.
You forced her face in the soapy sink water.
Pushing down. Down. Halfway to lonely
resolution and half way to never ending hell
but you pressed down deeper. Her lack of
struggle is her final gift to you.
But don't you worry jealous man.
She's still going to hold your hand
and speak softly to you into the early
morning fog and hold you and kiss your
forehead while you are sleeping and love
you in every way you don't deserve.

SARA DUST

You lived and died when the world was still free and burning.
I would gladly repay you with my flesh if you would only come down
from that high guard post you watch me from. You could lay me down as
if we were both equals. Every night I long to touch you even though I
have no right to.

You've seen all my faces , all my tricks and all my petty evil but you must
have seen some good or you would have abandoned me as a child. Is it
wrong for me to love the one who watches over me ?
Who have you destroyed to keep me breathing?
Would you.. Could you make me wait until the very end for your perfect
touch? I've seen your sweet perfection in my dreams and
no mortal woman could ever satisfy me now. Would god clip your wings
and curse the both of us if we broke the unspoken law ?
I would gladly be damned with you. Just reveal yourself now .
Please ! My hand is open and waiting for yours. Let's just run away.
I could protect you for a while. We could take the midnight train to
Chicago. Let's get lost in the big city. God would never find us there.
Baby don't make me beg..

How stupid am I? Or maybe too ambitious.
Trying to sleep with guardian angels is a very lonely game.

I AM YOUR JEALOUS LOVER

If I could only pull you from the card stock.
Two dimensional temptress. My flat and naked lover looking
deeper than I could ever hope to be. She'll soon be sold and leave
her master. Traveling to far off romantic places I can only wet dream
about. It is because she is the most beautiful that she leaves me quicker
than the other women of my life. She'll even last longer but
I can forgive her for that. After all, the world is for loving and letting
go... Including yourself.

I never pretended to own a woman. I know I was only a humble
custodian of that priceless beauty. It's true I worshiped daily. I protected
and tried to satisfy with blood and sweat but ultimately every great work
of art must be packaged up and sent abroad to another museum with
another lonely joke of a man who may or
may not know that he too is only the next humble custodian of
her love.

Sweet, shy and silent. You carefully watch me as I caress your thin
rectangle body. You smell of dirty acrylic water and my own sweaty
palms. How could I even start to understand the totality of what our love
meant or what I should have but could not do to keep you.

When you ran away I followed your tears and finally found you but you
had drowned in a lake of your own making. Face down floating in your
own man made alter of suicide and personal anguish. I tried to swim
those bitter tears but instead of bringing your body back to the shore I
decided to continue searching for you in the place death could only take
me.

HIGHWAY GHOSTS

When your car stalls out on the deserted highway, ghosts come a running. A dead cell and a couple stuck together pennies become sickly ironic like echoes of your own demented poetry thrown back at you. The highway prince a distant mirage slowly stumbles into view. Morning mist and rolling highway trash the metaphoric spirit drifters that seem to rob you. You quickly climb inside and secure the doors and windows. Mechanics with smoke faces pop your hood and rattle your frame. Through the eerie radio noise you hear "CCCRAAANNKK …. IIITTTT" You cannot breathe but you turn the key. The sound is your rapture and you're back on the Bloody Pass again.

YOUR NAKEDNESS

I want you to show
me something I would kill for.
Die for. Live for and lie for.
Show me the truth I've been running
from. Remind me that I'm still a man.
Remind me that I'm not dreaming.
Can I be the breath you're breathing?
Can I be the blood your perfect
heart is beating? I need you to
show me what you keep vulnerable
and sacred. I long to be your carnal slave.
I long to be your disrobed shadow, your
arousing little secret.

So why can't you long for me as I do you?
Why can't you bend to my will?
Why can't you just bend over the bed?

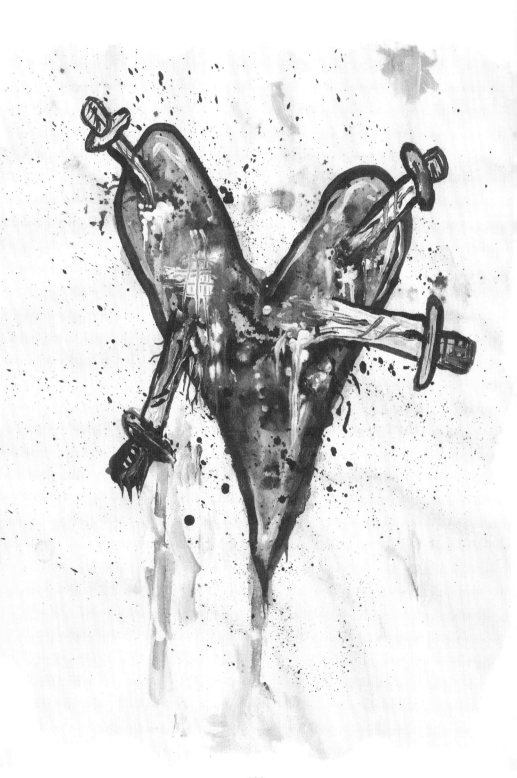

LOVE IS

It's been proven and tested over the ages.
These universal truths, simple and solid.
Love is crazy. Love is deadly.
Love is suicide. Love is worthwhile.

ZOMBIE CONTENDERS

Reanimated were the empty suits.
All in pursuit of a frightened woman.
Tear drop seeds of poison panic.
A pitch black rush into the open darkness.
The night hides our imminent death encircling around.
Rip through the gravel parking lot.
Quickly now. Hungry sounds.
Corpse army trail behind on foot.
Like a Lynch movie the meaning misunderstood.
Out of fuel. Now we're fucked.
Cannibal companions gather to contend for her love.
Searching through sweet flesh and bone to find some.

NECROCOMMANDER

He's the one that controls the bass.
Thug mystic. Heliophobic Ace.
Raw sex is pumping and speaking on beat.
Whores accrue and join the scene.
Warning. Warning.
Voices amplified from Heaven.
God is bounced quickly at the door.
Angels fly down to settle the score.
John the Revelator's platinum binoculars pierce the night.
Songs are woven and spun brandishing his audible might.
The undead prepare to kiss and touch.
The great meat market winds down around five o'clock.
When the night is through his legions must retire.
The wastrels scatter and the black-robed
vultures descend again upon Tel Megiddo.

SADIE

I fell in love with a much older lady.
Didn't know her last name but the first was Sadie.
I felt like a dog because she never asked me to speak.
When she took her clothes off for me I could not even think.
God. I loved Sadie and the forbidden things she taught me.
If I knew where she was now not a living man could stop me.
Sadie my love, I'll never stop looking for you and if the
Grim Reaper took you then have him drop by my house too.

IN LOVE

We used to be in love.
When love was just a word.
But now that love means love.
The word is scarcely heard.

When you said I love you.
I knew you felt obliged.
But it made me happy anyway.
The devotion in your lie.

I want to thank you for your deceit.
Even though you don't give a damn.
Your deception kept me living.
And that's a truth I'll always have.

EED WAS ~~HERE~~

Gotta watch it.
He's gonna put me away.
Burning the holy places where I play.
He bombed out the carnival that was my mind.
The cunning devil I hide behind.
The suffocating clay in which I swim.
A greasy serpent full of sin.
A rotten lemon I have to bite.
A nose full of scat.
Illegal cock-fight.
All the things that will put me away.
He proudly presents them to the world today.

INDEX OF TITLES

JUSTIN AERNI was born in Arizona in 1984. His artistic career began in 2006 when he started exhibiting his work in galleries and selling it online. He is also the author and illustrator of such books as ; *"Fighting For Fiction"* - 2008 *"Nonsense Relevant"* - 2009 and *"Dead Business Men"* , a graphic novel in 2009 . To date Aerni has created and sold over 2000 paintings to collectors worldwide and has been featured in numerous art and culture magazines .

2833831R00074

Printed in Great Britain
by Amazon.co.uk, Ltd.,
Marston Gate.